THE  POWER OF

THE

VOICE

FIND, REGAIN, AND USE
YOUR UNIQUE SOUND

James Vincent

THE POWER OF THE VOICE
FIND, REGAIN, AND USE YOUR UNIQUE SOUND
2nd edition

Published by

James Vincent III

Printed in USA

©2016, 2023 James Vincent III

ISBN-13: 978-0-9986413-6-2

ISBN-10: 0-9986413-6-1

The web addresses mentioned in this book were functional at the time of publication; however, we bear no responsibility for their accessibility or inaccessibility.

To my loving wife, Robyn, and my children,
Traclyn, Raven, Jamyn, Shira-Sion, Justice,
and everyone and everything that has either
loved me, hated me, helped me, or hindered
me... you all help me find my voice.

Chapter 1
SILENCE

Herman grew up in a fairly large, blended family, six children in all in the home, with his father and step-mother. He was ten years old when his birth-mother and father divorced; upon receiving the news of the divorce, he and his two younger brothers wept sorely. Up until that point, they'd been extremely close with their mother, having lived with her through a separation, but now they were to live full-time with their father, whom they mainly knew at the time as a quite frightening disciplinarian.

Herman's mother eventually told him the date the divorce was to be finalized, and he watched daily in doleful anticipation of this deeply deplorable family dissolution. When it finally arrived, he approached his father in tears.

"What are you crying about?" his father asked.

"Today is the day you and Mama are getting a divorce."

His father, presumably unwittingly, gave a most callous response. "Boy, that doesn't have anything to do with you. And anyway, it's not until tomorrow."

The end.

To make a long story short, from those days into his adulthood, Herman lived his life holding in his deepest emotions. His childhood would be filled with many awful issues that he'd not feel the freedom to express to anyone. He would have passionate bursts of anger every now and then when situations in his life hit an uncontainable boiling point. He had a generally calm personality, however; he was good at keeping his mouth shut and pleasing those around him. This made it quite easy for people to get what they wanted out of him, practically walking all over him as if his own voice didn't matter. In those rare moments that he did express himself, it appeared to others as though he were acting "out of character."

Herman grew up, got married, had children. He'd feel at many times the need to fight for respect in his own home; the frustrations of his childhood manifesting in ugly ways toward his family.

This issue of the voice is one that is near to my heart. One of the truest and most interesting things I have found concerning the voice is that the fact that someone speaks does not necessarily equate having a voice. There are individuals who happen to be deaf and/or mute whose voice and purpose have been greatly felt in our time. As we delve into the heart of this subject, understand that your voice is linked with your purpose, your reason for being.

In this book, I hope to appeal to a part of you other than your intellect. I am not a psychologist or expert in pathology; I am a regular guy like you who has walked through and is still walking on this journey of finding my true voice. Using what I've learned, I do my best to help others release their fears or whatever inner issues ail them and help them free their own voices, without the confusing, intellectual jargon. You'll find later as you continue to read that we don't always process well the inner part of us through our brains; yet we seem to think every solution will come by changing or addressing something *outward*. Intellect is more outward than inward, and the same way we use topical medications to address inner physical issues, let your intellect be more of the "avenue of entry" instead of the answer to your issues. And typically, if you start with the innards, the outward follows suit.

"Innards." Ha! I like that word.

I am a musician, singer, and speaker by profession. I have done voiceover work. I am bilingual and can communicate somewhat effectively in a few other languages. My voice is extremely important when it comes to what I do. If I didn't have a physical voice, I would definitely have to consider an alternate line of work. For years, however, although I sang and touched many hearts, I still had a very suppressed personality. There was a silence on the inside that controlled my emotions and responses to life in general. Even at times when I knew it was right for me to speak up, I'd convince myself that what I had to say either wasn't important or that it would only cause trouble. I'd "go along with the program", much like Herman in the story we read earlier, to please those around me. Is anything inherently wrong with any of these things I listed? It is certainly good to know when and when not to speak up, when not to stir up trouble, when to simply go along with the program and keep your mouth shut; I truly believe that. But I, like many who may be reading this, filtered *everything* through the lens of keeping silent.

What is silence? Is silence simply the absence of sound? Is silence simply not speaking up when you should? Why don't we take a deeper look.

One of the definitions of silence in the Merriam-Webster dictionary is **oblivion; obscurity**. **Oblivion** connotates something that is forgotten, not used, or even thought about; it's also the state of being altogether dazed or unaware of the world around you. **Obscurity,** in simplest terms, is more or less being in an *unknown or unclear* state. So in effect, when I decided to keep my voice suppressed, I was boring a hole deeper and deeper into oblivion and obscurity. I had allowed this thought process to seep into and take over my outlook on life; to affect and shroud my purpose. Everything I did was overcast with a propensity to back down, become discouraged, not take risks, be someone different in public than I was when I was alone. My development was arrested, opportunities were missed, and I walked through many tribulations because of this. My very nature became confused between what I truly was and what I was trying to reduce myself to. Obscurity.

We all have a purpose, an ultimate reason for our existence, whether we want to believe it or not. Much of our quality of modern life has to do with hundreds, thousands of years of people walking out their life's purpose. Many of us don't know Martin Cooper's name, but most of the world experiences his efforts daily when we use our cell phones. Imagine someone like him saying, "Gee, it sure would be great if I could use a phone on the go, and not need to be confined to one location in order to communicate with whomever I want. But… naaah. That's dumb. It'll never happen; and even if it did, it would never be accepted into society. Let me spend my time on something more important, like watching TV. TV… now *that's* quite an invention." It sounds silly, but it's something many of us do regularly; I know I have. Not that I could have or would have invented something like a cell phone, but I'd developed a habit of kicking out thoughts or imaginations that took me beyond my then-current processes. I had developed a habit of silence.

It is extremely difficult to discover one's true voice if it is continually suppressed. As Herman learned, the negative implications can be life-altering, and for years one can be held in a prison of oblivion with not the slightest idea or hope of getting free. Yes, many times the "hush" is self-inflicted; other times, it is forced and/or taught even by a sometimes well-meaning authority, whether father, mother, boss, church leader, teacher, etc.

I once found myself apologizing to my now adult twin daughters for treating them like they had no voice. Because I was raised a certain way, I felt that because they were children, their thoughts didn't really count. So, I took their words with a grain of salt and made them shut up when I felt that what I had to say was more important. Now don't get me wrong– I am an advocate of children learning to be quiet and listen to authority without having an argumentative response. But that isn't what I'm talking about. I'm talking about the mentality that says, "I'm right because I'm grown, you're wrong because you're a child; so just shut up and take what I say." I have become a proponent of healthy conversation within the boundaries of child-to-parent respect, as the parent also realizes that that child is a real person with real feelings and real questions.

And yes, to all you other parents out there- there are those times where they do need to shut up and do as they are told.

One fear that many parents have is giving their children a negative response, specifically saying "no." They think that "no" will produce a negative life outlook and, for the sake of this book, a silence within them. Then they are more and more discouraged to go after what they desire because they are afraid of or are expecting a negative response. While I understand that argument, I completely disagree. I believe that we must teach our children that there will be negative responses in life, but that does not mean to stop going after what we want. I tell my children all the time, "Don't be afraid to ask. Sometimes I'll say yes, sometimes, I'll say no. But still... ask." And I'll tell you what... they ask, ask, ask, ask. And they also ask.

The manner in which we give our children a negative response, however, does matter. I don't just say, "NO! Get outta here! Stupid question!" I'll say,

13

"No, why don't you go do this; or, no, it's too early; or no, not today; no, that's not for children your age." And sometimes, no is simply no; they've learned that there are times when that is just the way it is. My children are the *least* silent children you will find, however. I find sometimes that I have to come a bit outside of my parameters to keep up with their freedom to be who they are! Of course, "no" is not the answer they always receive. Affirmative responses are just as important as negative responses; I believe all children should learn to receive both. Raising children is a task, especially attempting to raise them to be different than yourself. But *healthily* raising them to have a voice– when you haven't fully found yours– is an arduous undertaking.

I realize that some who are reading this book are not yet or may never be a parent; however, there is *someone* you will influentially impact. We will either have positive or negative impact; either help move forward or be a stumbling block. Neutrality, for the most part, is oblivion, so let's throw that out of the window for now. Your voice *will affect someone.* Silence should never be our end goal, nor should it be anyone's lot in life. Who's to say where African Americans would be in the USA without an influential voice like Martin Luther King? How would his cause have been affected if he'd have reverted to silence, succumbing to negativity and discouragement? I can guarantee that many of his followers would have followed suit, while others would have either angrily picked up a new torch or sunk deeper into oppression. But his voice was so inspirational that even after his tragic death, his words remain as a hope to all mankind. Trust me, I have heard his words quoted all over the world.

All of this having been said, I think it's safe to assume that if one is not living out the true purpose for which he was born, he is living in a state of silence. Remember, to be oblivious is to be in a *dazed-like state*, and I believe that we are floating in a kind of limbo-false reality when we consistently allow our true voice to come under the suppression and oppression of undue silence.

For years, I worked in construction. Over time, I had acquired many skills that varied from pouring concrete, to plumbing, to remodeling homes. I remember being hired as a helper with one company after I had moved to a new city and had been looking for work. I knew that my experience was better than just being a helper, but I didn't mind. I wasn't one to toot my own horn, and besides, it was a job. Well, this kid I worked under was as slow. as. molasses. He was also meticulous with things that anyone with experience would have known didn't matter. But, since I was the helper, I didn't fuss, didn't try to teach him; I just followed his instructions. After a few hours, I began to *feel* like a helper. I became unsure of whether to do one thing or the other without instruction. My years of experience took a back seat to my present state.

Because we worked so slowly, we were both told after a couple of days that we weren't needed any longer. Had I found a way to be more vocal about how we could be more efficient, and not played the "humility game", I would not have been let go. My silence lost me that job; but not only was I silent, I began to *"wear"* what the silence was producing in me: inexperience, timidity, confusion...

Thank God a couple of days later I received a call from that company. Someone there had vouched for me and said, "No, James was only following that other guy's instructions. He's a good worker." Needless to say, I wasn't shy about making my skill level known after that. I held a job with them until they went out of business, and when the manager started his own business, I was one of the only ones he asked to work for him. Not long after, I started my own business doing construction, and it was my non-silence that won me jobs. I had to come to another level of being vocal; another level of confidence about who I was and what I did. I have since dissolved that business, but I'd sold myself so well that I still have former clients calling for my services to this day! Now, it's still not my personality to toot my own horn, but I don't allow a tendency towards obscurity to be something that holds me back. Take a moment and think: what is your silence losing for you at this very moment?

Let's return to our character, Herman. Remember his calm personality that would at times explode into episodes of anger? Much of that anger accumulated because of missed opportunities to speak up. When people would walk over him, hold him back because of things they'd assumed about him, treat him as though he didn't truly matter, he would allow those lying voices to build up inside of him instead of combating the adversity with the reality of who he was. The safest assumption in this case would be that Herman was not in touch with his true identity. The inflicting silence created a kind of concealment; his voice wasn't able to speak out against what was arresting him because essentially, he'd never used that voice. Herman had no comprehension of the things that continually either slipped through his fingers or remained just out of reach simply because he had no voice.

Eventually, Herman would become content in "circling the mountain" over and over; it was what he had become accustomed to as opportunities would come and go. He would watch others reach out with fiery fervor and determination for the things they'd endeavor to accomplish, while he wished and wondered what it was that made things attainable for them. Why was it so difficult for him to do the same?

As I alluded to a bit earlier, the issue of the voice goes so much deeper than a sound created by air and vibrations of the larynx; it is more than what people hear when you open your mouth to speak, sing, shout. It is inseparably linked to your identity; the purpose for which you were born. Undue, entrapping, enslaving silence actively works against that purpose, and we eventually find ourselves stifled, with a near-inability to properly use our voice to rise above that dark cloud. Without the right realizations and inner strengthening, it can be hard to climb our way out of such a profound black hole.

How deep does it go?

Chapter 2
VOICE RAIDERS: THE
SILENCE BEGINS

I was part of a musical event recently, and my youngest son, who at the time of my writing this is five years old, was standing in the front row with my wife and began to dance and move to the sound without inhibition. Most of us feel the desire to engage in some sort of motion when we hear a compelling rhythm, but this was different. How, you ask? He was the *only* one dancing. Everyone else was spectating, as it actually was a kind of spectating moment. I watched him move almost to the center aisle, when my wife's and my eyes met. We grinned instantaneously at each other as we both knew that we didn't really want to stop him from expressing what was on the inside of him. I then motioned from the stage for her to move him out of the aisle. She proceeded to move him, but he sat down, thinking that's what she wanted.

"Oh no!" I thought to myself, as I saw him kind of sink into a still, repressive kind of a lull. We hadn't wanted him to stop, we'd just wanted him not to be disruptive. I wanted so badly to jump off of the stage and dance with him at that point, to re-fan whatever smoldering ember was still remaining inside of him to wiggle to his little heart's content.

As I thought about that moment later on, I was taken back to my early childhood years. I remembered being at my uncle's wedding at age eight, and there was upbeat music playing. The dance floor was empty except for one person-- me. I couldn't help but move to the music. I moved the way I felt; young, carefree, vibrant. No one stopped me from dancing, and I imagine some people got quite a kick out of watching me. However, I wasn't aware of being watched; I just expressed freely who I was in that moment.

Reflecting on those things caused me to question why I wasn't that free any longer. I understood that I had reached a mature age, and that I didn't process things the way I did as a child; but that *should* be the case for any adult. What should *not* be the case is that we lock away or lose that childlike part of us that knows when to stop taking life so seriously; that part that knows how to easily let go. When I lost that, in essence, I lost my freedom. I had become a type of prisoner to whatever would afford me any feeling of freedom; I had given control of my voice to those things.

Among the terrible things about giving away control of your voice is that either (1) you are controlled by fear of others and easily conform in order to gain their approval, or (2) you are prone to responding negatively to a person or situation that you feel is attacking your individuality. I mention these two issues together, because they are essentially the same issue on "opposite poles", if you will. It is almost common knowledge in today's society that someone who is self-confident will not likely have a strong tendency toward either of these issues. There is a kind of resident liberty within him that allows for a more even, confident approach to human interaction.

Now, I'm not addressing the hundreds, even thousands of things we tend to battle within ourselves in addition to the voice issue– erratic behavior, depression, *aggression*, *talking too much,* etc.– all things that come into play whether we are afflicted with silence issues or not. But many of us experience certain personality "demons" *as a result* of our vocal prison.

Much like Herman, whom we mentioned in chapter one, our vocal prisons can likely root from some event or series of events during our upbringing. Herman was missing a certain element of love and validity that caused his voice to become suppressed after the issue of divorce ravaged his world. Before his voice could be loosed from that deep, silent vacuum, the issue of his anger would need to be addressed with an affirming love that would help to melt away the hard shell that covers the true being of a person. That anger he would project in times of pressure and adversity became a kind of mask that would continually compound the intensity of the unaddressed, underlying issues that produced that anger. We will discuss this "mask" in later chapters. Although his anger would make him *loud* at times, he still suffered from a voice that was being held captive, not realizing that he was acting out of past pain and scars; this would be an example of personality "demons" that *cause* a vocal prison.

An interesting study is how our personalities are shaped by our environment, not only as children, but even into adulthood. We learn, respond, relate many times because of what is afforded to us in our atmosphere. What types of things do we consistently hear? What do we see that forms how we view things? What have we experienced in life that causes us to respond in different ways? I've known people who have heard nothing but negative words spoken to them, like, "You sing like a sick cat," or, "You're not as smart as your sister," or, "You'll never amount to anything in life." Believe it or not, these types of soul-cursing environments are very common.

Hopelessness and failure without recourse grip the imaginations of those reared in these settings, because all they've ever heard is that they are *incapable*. It really is a shame how some people who really seem to have a good head on their shoulders have such a hard time speaking up for themselves, overcoming adversity, or even making a simple decision. Often times there is no control over their emotions, becoming confused, depressed, or angry, not knowing how to turn negativity into positive energy.

On the other hand, there are those raised in a relatively nurturing setting and hearing things like,

"Great job," or, "You can be anything you want to be," or even receiving attention that makes them feel they are worth something. Most of these people seem better equipped to handle life in general; they don't internalize failure or negativity, but learn how to overcome it. They figure out how to clearly articulate what is happening within themselves and have better control over their emotions. Silence for many of them is a circumstantial choice, not a state of being.

One of my lingering issues that has popped up every now and then is remaining silent at certain times in order to keep peace, whether peace needed to be kept or not. I just didn't want anything bad happening to me, or *as a result* of me releasing my voice. As I searched deeply within myself (and prayed as well; as a Christian, that's what I do), I found that at the root of my keeping quiet in many instances was fear. Now that is probably not a huge revelation for many of us to "stop the presses" (or should I say *"uploads"* for modern times); however, fear comes in many times through some opening within us that gives way to it. In other words, *why am I fearful??* What happened in my life that causes me to continually be controlled by fear in certain instances? And don't necessarily equate fear with being scared or afraid; think of fear as an inordinate hesitation that grips your normal processes and attempts to control them.

I travel all over the world, and I have the privilege of experiencing various cultures. I traveled to Kenya and noticed that the general population carried themselves in a rather stuffy manner. I knew a bit about the history of that country, and I guessed that (no harm intended) this was because of the British influence. I was relieved to hear that many Kenyans felt the same way, so it wasn't offensive for them to hear me suggest something like that. Then, one of my Kenyan friends took me a little deeper into some of their history.

When the British colonized Kenya, he said, they began to address much of the indigenous culture, deeming it less than genteel. They made a more than successful attempt to cause the Kenyans to assimilate their own cultural ways. Because the British were Christian, part of their mission was to evangelize. Being a Christian myself, I didn't see evangelism as an entirely bad thing; however, there was a less than subtle constriction in their approach.

My friend told me that one of their tactics was to force the Kenyans to stop playing their native instruments, causing them to believe that those instruments were of the devil. With that, the larger part of society neglected the sounds that were birthed from within their own DNA, and adopted a foreign sound; in essence, their sound was squeezed out, captured, and superseded by something less than what they were meant to create. To this day, although the British no longer rule there, there is still an atmosphere of oppression that seems to linger. Aside from the few who work to preserve the culture, it's like their true identity has been lost in the silence. The fear that twists many all over the world into a perverted sense of existence is the same fear that resides in places like Kenya.

So here I was, a grown man, longing once again to be that free, fearless little boy without a care in the world, floating on the clouds of lightsome skies. As I reflected on life events that had a damaging effect on my inner liberty, I thought of others I had known who had experienced and suffered through things that shut down their voices. I knew of one young lady who had been raped as a teenager by her older cousin. She told her mother about the atrocity she had experienced, but her mother did nothing. The young lady expressed that she felt she couldn't say anything to anyone else police, school officials, or even her father, because she was made to feel that somehow the rape was her fault.

She moved past that horrific event, grew up, got married, had children. There would be many things that would happen in her life that would cause her to feel oppressed, trapped, and even violated. In several of those cases, she would keep her inner torture to herself, because hey, *it was probably her fault she felt violated anyway. And besides, no one would do anything about it if she did speak up.* Many cases like these prove to end with grave results, but as hope would have it, she had a generally upbeat personality that didn't allow her to live in a continual oppressed state. It was in specific instances that she'd battle that demon. Not all of us are quite as fortunate, being almost completely overcome in all areas of our lives by the thing that silences us.

The story I just told, while all too common, is approaching some of the more extreme cases I've heard. But what about the subtle "voice raiders" that leave you wondering years later, *"Who the heck is this person looking back at me in the mirror??"*

Chapter 3
VOICE RAIDERS: THE
CONFORMITY CLAUSE

So many of us as children start out with dreams, whether big, small, outlandish, unrealistic, or attainable. My youngest daughter said she wanted to be a singer (like her father), a dancer, a doctor, and a princess, while my youngest son proudly proclaimed that he wanted to be a skunk. Yes... a *skunk*. I had a good laugh on that one, but I didn't tell him that there was no way he could actually attain skunkhood; he'll eventually figure that out in his own. But what I do with my daughter is help her develop her talent by singing fun songs with her, encouraging her to sing in her school talent shows, letting her sing on my recordings, etc. I want her to know that her dream is attainable, whether she becomes a princess or not.

As for being a doctor, there are avenues and protocols that must legally be followed in order to be able to legitimately practice that profession; after all, it's people's lives and trust we're talking about. My daughter would need to have the fervency and confidence to reach that goal, and if being a doctor is what she really wants to do, she needs to know that she can do it, and that those who matter are behind her one hundred percent. I would let her know though that in order to become a legally practicing doctor, these are the things that you must do.

What I won't do is tell her that in order to become a singer or dancer or whatever else, she must do it the way Daddy did it. We seem to have a worldwide epidemic that seems to affect even the most obscure crevices of civilization: that in order to attain a particular goal, we must do it *this* way. Work really hard. Go to college. Audition for that. It seems that only a select few who break out of a mold truly make an impact on society. What we tend to do to each other is base our futures on what has already passed, and possibly thwart any individual progression into true, unique greatness.

It's a very touchy subject, because we have been so trained to process life in a very specific way. I mentioned college, so let's dwell there for a moment. Education is an important process that affords us a good basis of relating in the modern world; however, most of what, why, and how we learn today is based on a few "intelligent" men that decided what was best for everyone. Much of our schooling is simply built on variations of their principles. So instead of receiving building blocks that help us create our world, we are sculpted into someone else's way of processing things.

I read a very insightful book, "Ungifted: Intelligence Redefined", by Scott Barry Kaufman, that highlighted the fact that our universal method for schooling and learning are generally built for one type of learner. The avenues for determining who is gifted, who is average, and who is "slow" are based on this one method. If you excel in that method, or exceed expectations, you are awesome. If you don't show proficiency within that method, something isn't right. Perhaps you're not quite as intelligent as others and need "special education." Or perhaps consider a career collecting trash, because you may not do well in anything that requires much more of you. Now listen, I personally believe the job of collecting trash is very respectable; but sometimes we accept a particular position in life because we are made to think by "higher minds" that we aren't made to fit in another position.

With that in mind, we already have so many examples of people who have transcended the status quo and became huge successes. Somehow, they figured out that there was something more on the inside of themselves than what the "rat race" could provide, they *believed* it, then took a leap of faith. But I, like many others, found it a hopelessly impossible task to even figure out whatever "leap of faith" personally meant to me. There was obviously some disconnect that had snuck upon me over time; a part of me that had been lost somewhere between, "you can do anything," and, "what are you going to do with your life?"

My father worked his way through college, alternating between going to school for a semester, then taking off a semester to make money, and finished by the time I was born. My mother returned to school later in life and received her degree by the time I was around 14 years old. Both showed a resilience and determination in completing what they felt was necessary to do in order to survive and provide for our family. Although they both moved and operated with excellence according to the system they knew, they stood on opposite sides of the spectrum concerning my education. While my mother believed that I should receive a decent, viable education in a subject that would help me get a well-paying job, my father believed that I should learn about something that I loved. I loved music.

It wasn't that my mother didn't want me to be a musician; she wanted me, in her words, "to have something to fall back on" in case I wasn't a successful one, or wasn't able to sufficiently support my family as a musician. As a mother, she wanted me to succeed in life and not struggle the way others had had to struggle. My father's words to me, however, were, "Well, do you plan on falling back?" His words helped me decide to choose music as my university major. I met my wife not long after, and married her before finishing school. Because of my fear of accumulating too much debt, I dropped out; exiting one "rat race" to enter another. I worked very hard to support my family, learning useful skills that gave me enough knowledge to eventually start my own handyman business. Throughout this time, however, there was a nagging insecurity that continually reared its tortuous head: I was a failure for not finishing college.

There are many things in our lives that seem to be defined by our surroundings, by modern society, by media; it's only natural that we are influenced by the world we know. But many times, we become captured by the era's measuring stick for success, and true potential gets lost in what we've been conditioned to accept as normal- or highest achievable- life. Because I felt I wasn't meeting this status quo, I thought I was failing at life, and cheating my family out of their best life possible. I mean, my parents were college graduates. Many of my cousins, aunts, and uncles were degreed and successful. Why was I not doing my best to jump into the "way of the world" and secure my own family's future in this competitive life circus?

Here is my personal conviction: as a parent, it's my responsibility to help my children get on a path to reach their individual, full potential. Keeping in mind that they do need to relate to the world around them, my wife and I emphasize to our children that there is something unique within each one of them that should take them far beyond what we, or anyone else for that matter, can teach them. We make an effort to teach them what we know so that they have useful tools to begin their journey on a higher plane than we did. The mistake I was making (before I finally got a clue) was thinking that everyone MUST start from the bottom and work their way up to achieve what someone else had already achieved. That was just life; it's the cycle most of the world falls into. This is why the world is advanced by a select few innovators while the rest of us say, "I wish I would have thought of that," then go back to daydreaming about unfulfilled dreams. I literally watched my oldest son become me, kind of wandering through life and walking in circles within his own world. At first, I wondered why he looked lost, without purpose, and in effect, gripped by deafening silence. Then I realized that what I was seeing was my own mirror image; he was aimless because *I* was aimless. I was aimless because in the deepest crevices of my soul, I had no idea who I was or why I was even walking this earth. I hadn't learned many useful things from my father (though he was a good father), and psychology will tell you that that is a recipe for lifelong meandering.

So I took an inventory of my life. Where am I? How did I get here? What have I learned along the way? What have I gained or lost during this journey? How can I use these things to "invade" my child's world in order to prevent him from entering the cycle of assimilation and aimlessness? How can I use these things to help *myself* out of this rut? I didn't realize until then how much I had to offer my children besides love and attention; and I basically began to force my son (he was a teenager after all) to learn the things that I know. As I said before, he will find his own way; but he will begin on a higher plane, with direction and purpose. And he will thank me when he is an adult.

Pouring myself into my son gave me a new sense of being and caused me to recognize the rich, deep well that I had within me. Dreams that had long since faded began to reawaken. I decided that I would allow those dreams to take form again and never have them squeezed out of me by what status quo has caused me to believe is or is not achievable by me. I had to get above every opposing attitude or thing that would attempt to dictate any viability or non-viability of my dreams. I purposed to set myself on the offensive against the silencers that would otherwise cause a regression into the world I had already felt I was failing in.

Without delving too deeply into spirituality, I will say that it is interesting to see how much we are shaped by such a partial, limited view of the world we live in. I don't think we realize how we allow that limited view to become the basis for how we process *everything*. It defines what we see as beautiful, who we think is intelligent or uncivilized, what things we give value to. I discovered that I had set up a mental shrine for this dream of getting a college degree so that I could be worth something in this world; not realizing that I was neglecting all of the other things inside of me that were presently already worth something. I thought, "The world puts value on that college degree; therefore, with that degree, I am valuable." Although I was very gifted and could do just about anything, I'd let myself become ensnared by this partial mentality.

Now, I'm not saying that nobody needs a college degree; I'm saying that I was living below my potential because I was thinking according to the things the world puts value on, and not causing myself to blossom out of my own God-given inner worth. Once I realized that this world was so much bigger than another man's standard, I felt that much more liberty to just... be.

Like my Kenyan friend expressed to me, the pure, indigenous sound of Kenya was lost, at least in the Christian world, because someone came in and told them that their instruments and sounds were of the devil. It wasn't because the British had heard God say that the sounds were demonic; it was because they wanted to impose the world *they* knew upon that culture. So just like that, the Kenyans adopted someone else's partial world view that would mask the fullness of who they were and diminish what they could produce as a unique people with a unique voice. It's kind of sickening when you think about it, don't you think?

Nothing against the Brits. Some of my good friends are British.

Such is the detriment of what I have deemed the "conformity clause". Most of us have experienced it, whether we have succumbed to it or transcended it. The conformity clause guarantees you some level of success and freedom, as long as you come under a level of restriction and duplication. I believe this has created a huge handicap worldwide, cheating us all out of the beauty that makes each individual who they are. At times this clause is forced upon us; other times, it is presented as the only plausible option when we desire to move ahead in some area of life. And trust me- I understand that sometimes, we've just "gotta do what we gotta do" to get through some situations- but many times it's because everyone is taught that the way(s) they know happen to be the *only* way(s).

There are many absolutes in this world we know. Things like rape, as an extreme example, we know are absolutely wrong, no two ways about it. For me, whatever the word of God spells out is absolute. Water in liquid form is absolutely wet. The complete absence of light is absolute darkness. I think many of our major problems with some of our government and school systems has to do with not defining absolutes. However, things like killing another human being may be entirely circumstantial. Morality in this case may depend on the situation (war, self defense, cold-blooded murder), and may even be left to interpretation. People like me who struggled for so long to find their voice have often found themselves fighting a world of absolutes where they did not apply. Yet, in order to remain safe, we allowed our voice to become shaped- or in the least, *imprisoned-* by that world. This is what makes me appreciate people like "plus-size" models. But what is a plus-size model anyway? What makes them plus-size? Society's interpretation of what regular-size is? So in some instances, these people have shown that they are comfortable in their skin, and that the world doesn't dictate to them what real beauty is.

The first thing I had to do to break free from the conformity clause was to stop fearing the repercussions of taking that leap [of breaking free]. *"What if they don't like me? What it I lose something? What if my dignity is affected? What if this, what if that, what if, what if, what IF???"* This seems to be the one thing that keeps us from breaking free of whatever is holding us in conformity when we want to de-conform (is that a term?). I equate it to standing on the edge of a cliff, needing to get to the ground far below me. The only way I'll ever get to the bottom is to jump, but I keep looking at all the reasons why I shouldn't do it. *"It's too far down; I'll hurt myself; no one has ever done this."* So what I intentionally do is [figuratively] cover my eyes and step off the ledge in order to get things in motion. Suddenly, there's no turning back; it may be messy, but I can't reverse things now- I'm in mid-air! It doesn't get *rid* of the "what if's"... it causes me to face them.

Someone once expressed to me that even deciding to "step off the ledge" was hard to do. I explained to that person that the reason they found it so hard was because they think there is something they need to figure out about it. They need every "what if" answered before they let go. Well, let me make this as clear as possible... *That's called not letting go.* They not only wanted the method of breaking free of whatever was holding them back, they wanted the method of letting go of the method! Again, the what ifs don't go away, but you create a much needed confrontation with fears and chains when you take that leap of faith. It's called a risk, and any good risk taker will tell you– there is no cut and dry method to risk-taking. That's why it's called a risk. (smile)

I also needed to realize that not all conformity is bad. This one is big. There are times that I will enter an unfamiliar arena, or an area where someone else knows more than I do. It's good to understand that even though I have a lot to offer, so do others. I don't know everything! Like I mentioned earlier in this chapter, if my daughter wants to be a doctor, she will need to go through the right avenues, and for a time, she'll need to conform so that her bigger picture for her life may be realized. So, I take on for a brief moment what I need to take on so that I can be useful to others, and so that in the long run I've gained a credibility in an area that I'd like to influence with my uniqueness.

I needed to understand that the world I live in just may not be the world the next person lives in; and I had to be OK with that, even if the next person wasn't OK with it. So many of us are simply ready to drop all that we are just because someone shows disapproval of our voice. It may be hard to believe, but we all have something to offer. Your sound is important. The next guy's sound is important. Personally, I have had to (and still work to) stop interpreting and processing others' personalities through my own, and I've also had to stop letting people limit me according to their own understanding of what they think I should be. Be accommodating? Yes, of course... how are we all going to make it together? Compromise? Can't rule it out, after all, as

I said, I don't know everything. Make apologies for who I am at this point in life? Never.

As I have begun imparting these attitudes into my children, I have seen so much in myself that I've needed to unlearn. And I don't tell them things like, "you don't need college; that's someone else's way," but I teach them to know their own path, be comfortable with who God made them, be teachable, and have conviction about who they are and what they stand for. I let them know that their dreams are valid, and not to let life, circumstances, or other people's ways squeeze that out of them.

Chapter 4
VOICE RAIDERS:
GRIEF AND TRAUMA

*"Mutism is like a drug; it's so addictive...
You don't have to do anything."*

This is such a big issue; I dare not skip by this with a simple paragraph or two. The most detrimental captors of our voices are those that invade and ravage the very depths of our souls; things we may or may not realize have deeply affected us. Events that bring about grief and trauma in our lives can cause a lifetime of pain, fear, anger, and all sorts of negative emotions and life views that either trigger a misappropriation of our natural voice or cause silence (which are essentially the same thing).

One of the most pernicious cycles we can fall into is the cycle that continues because of our not knowing how to handle grief and the effects of traumatic issues. It's not the unfortunate events that cause the deepening spiral into the abyss of a nearlost identity and emotional prison, it's the fact that we aren't taught or shown how to walk through the issues in such a way that we still come out whole. Loss happens. Grief happens. Bad things happen to us; but we live in a world that is so full of disappointment, hurt, unfulfilled hopes, and people with their own grave issues that it can be nearly impossible to find the right road or person to help us heal in the correct way. What seems to happen is that we subconsciously create our own ways to deal with these things– most of these ways unhealthy– and we rarely come out without our soul still bleeding somewhere. There are things we've experienced that will likely leave scars that will remain until we leave this earth, *but it should never alter our identity in such a way that we are lost in obscurity forever*. Some good can actually come out of the process, and sometimes the process can help to reshape our voice for a new era of life we may be entering; but we first need to accept that process.

Dr. Chuck Pierce wrote an excellent chapter on moving through grief and loss in his book, "Possessing The Gates of Your Inheritance." In this chapter, one of the things he writes about is the heart-wrenching experience of losing his newborn twins. He states that although he went through a period of grieving for the twins, that the "process of healing from that trauma is still a reality" in his life. Proper grieving allows us to heal in such a way that we are not stuck in the traumatic moment longer than we need to be; it helps us to keep from parking in our moment of loss and building our lives and relationships *around* that loss. So Chuck allowed (and allows) himself to go through whatever process he needs to so that whatever unhealed areas need to be addressed will not remain a stumbling block to him. Here is a small excerpt from that chapter:

> *Deep hurts require deep healing. And the healing process is usually longer and more strenuous than we ever expect. In fact, counselors will often refer to a person in the midst of recovering from loss as doing "grief work." This is a term used to describe a conscious decision to experience the emotions of grief as they come-- no matter how uncomfortable they may be-- and see those emotions through to the end. The theory behind grief work is that as we allow ourselves to grieve through the ebb and flow of natural emotion, healing can begin to penetrate the pain. If we do not allow ourselves to heal and instead deny our emotions, the grief will fester and often*

*manifest later in various harmful ways
such as addictions, chronic depression,
fits of anger or even physical illness.*

As I said, somehow, many of us have not been
afforded an environment where we can learn to be led
through the emotional results of our negatively
impacting life events in such a way that it *adds to* us. So
every traumatic experience seems to steal a piece of our
voice– many times, *all* of our voice– and our true, natural
expression is shrouded by some other twisted thing, like
rage or depression. Others of us are sometimes not
willing to face the process, choosing to abide in a place
of deep wounding. Nothing around us changes; we're
still quiet and angry, but remain afraid to walk through
that uncomfortable place that will eventually lead us into
wholeness.

Our voice was created to be heard. Even if it's
not functioning the way it should, it doesn't negate the
fact that it was meant to create some sound. In the same
way, we were created with the ability to heal. We were
created with some intrinsic power to sustain injury, find
what we need to overcome that injury, and come through,
sometimes more resilient than before. It pains me
sometimes to see people who have every resource

available to them to get through what they need to get through, yet still choose to live as a shattered soul. There is something about them that either feels that they don't *deserve* better, they don't believe or trust that they will actually come out better on the other side, or in some cases, being better will be in some way a betrayal to someone else. In a way, we fight hard against nature by *not* allowing ourselves to enter or remain in a healing process. When these things affect our expression, sometimes we become so familiar with this "unnatural nature" we've adopted that it becomes comfortable; it feels normal.

The late Maya Angelou was a gifted writer and very influential voice in our time. I saw an interview where she spoke about a deeply horrific experience she'd had, where she'd been raped by her mother's boyfriend. As a result of this and some ensuing consequences, she entered what is called *selective mutism.* It's a silence that comes because of some trauma, where the affected has the *ability* to speak, but is so gripped by the trauma that he or she just succumbs to its oppression and shuts down. Ms. Angelou didn't speak for a very long time, but was encouraged by someone to read poetry out loud. She finally came out of it and began to use her voice again, but said in the interview that mutism, even in her old age, would still creep up on her when some traumatic situation would arise. She pretty much stated that it was a comfortable place. *"Mutism is like a drug,"* she said. *"It's so addictive... You don't have to* do *anything."* This selective mutism, she admitted, was like an escape. She had become so accustomed to reverting to silence that it became the easier thing to do than to face her fears. She said in that same interview that in order to combat the mutism, she had to force herself out of it by using her voice. She wouldn't let herself become comfortable in the silence because she knew its detriment.

In my own life, I have found that there are times I must do the opposite of whatever negative response wants to rear its head because of some past grief. Like Maya Angelou, I am intentional about not allowing some *thing* to control my voice. That doesn't mean I hide my emotions; like we read earlier in this chapter, we need to allow those emotions to find an outlet so that we can become better. What it does mean is that I recognize, or at least question, where the negativity may really be coming from, then choose not to let it rule me. I haven't *mastered* it quite yet, but my wife and kids will testify that I'm far from the man I was!

My advice to you here would be to ask yourself next time you feel your voice or expression being led by something unnatural, *why does this upset me? why do I clam up in situations like the one I'm in? why does this make me fearful? why do I find it so hard to forgive or move past a certain situation?* Then, become active in the healing process. Choose not to let yourself live in a state where some past experience has control over areas of your life that should be showing more vibrancy. And remember that *healing is natural.* Not healing is *un*natural. It's against nature not to heal, so if you find yourself unable to heal, find out *why.*

Unforgiveness-- One of the Deadliest Traumas

"What?" you ask. "Why on earth is unforgiveness considered traumatic? Perhaps whoever crossed me or perpetrated grief in my life caused me to be unforgiving, but the *experience* was traumatic, not the unforgiveness." May I suggest, that since we have established the fact that our bodies, physically and *meta*physically, are meant to heal, that every time you decide to harbor unforgiveness towards yourself, someone else, or whatever, you are creating a trauma within your soul. Your soul is the inward makeup of who are; it, like our voice, is shaped by our experiences, environment, and things that we allow to affect it. Like our voice, the soul can change based on those things. The trauma of unforgiveness combats and batters against the part of your being that wants to be whole; it should be an unwelcome guest in our souls. Scientific studies have shown that unforgiveness can be the underlying issue in the development of many sicknesses. (I encourage you to research that.) The same can be said for the effects of grief and trauma. If you are allowing yourself to hold on to some bitterness that is caused by an unwillingness to forgive, don't think for one second that you are truly free to express yourself in the fullest way possible; something has a grip on your soul. It will be difficult to find the fullness of your voice when you are allowing it to be controlled by this foreign force.

The process of allowing ourselves to face the causes of our "voice raiders" will lead us on a real path to finding and using our natural expression. Bad things happen– *very* bad things happen– but when we let go of our fears and face them head on with the intention of being better, then the reality of who we are will set in, and we will become more and more free to face whatever other underlying issues are contributing to the masking of our voice. DO NOT become comfortable in the

53

negative effects of trauma; master it, and it won't master you.

Chapter 5
FINDING YOUR VOICE:
PURPOSE AWAKENS

Purpose. Belonging. Identity. I mentioned in the first chapter that our voice is inseparably linked with our identity. Remember, just because your larynx is functional and you have the ability to produce sounds does not necessarily mean you have found your voice. If you don't know why you are here, why you were created, it will be very hard to appropriate the uniqueness of your voice.

Some of us, myself included, are on a continual journey of discovering ourselves and our purpose. I have a generally solid idea of why I'm here, but I am continually being redefined as I reach certain milestones in my life and relationships. But it serves to say that in my understanding and belief, there is no true, realized identity outside of Christ. Roll your eyes if you like, but it's what I have found on my journey. I have observed billionaires and successful people-- *influential* people-- who are defined by what they do and have, but not who they are. They are still searching and longing, ever coming up empty as they grasp for something that seems tauntingly out of reach. Walking with God has not been the easiest road, but it is a road that has taken me to points within myself that cause me to weep with thankfulness and wonder, because I know I'd never have gotten there any other way. Without this true, inner sense of being, we wander, wander, wander; and whether we reach success, notoriety, wealth, or whatever it is we *think* we're searching for, it never equates a definite finding of ourselves.

On the subject of my beliefs, (which by the way, if I hadn't considered that there would be more than just people who believe as I do reading this book, this chapter would only have been a couple of sentences!) I understand that in relation to my chapter on "the conformity clause", some of you may ask, *"Well, aren't you only following in something somebody 'spoon-fed' you and made you think was true?"* And my answer to that would be, *yes...* at least that's kind of how it started. Honestly, I was a church goer because of my family. Then, something happened; something nobody forced on me or convinced me of. I began to develop my own love and vigor within my life for the things that I'd heard and seen. And then I started having my *own* experiences. No one brainwashed me or made me do anything except go to church. When I strayed, no one convinced me to return– it was something greater. (We know all too well the stories of people who started out in church and ended up nowhere near it!) It was bigger than me.

One of our major pitfalls is that in our search, we search *solely for our own fulfillment.* If you are going to find your purpose, you've got to grasp the mindset of living for something greater than yourself. What good are you if you're only here for *you??* That ought to wake some of us up right there. Some of us live to bring hope to others, while others of us live to give back to and advance society. Whatever it is, it must cause you to focus more outwardly than inwardly. It seems like a kind of paradox, but it's right.

As I entered fatherhood, I found that when my first son was born, I wanted to share everything with him. Up until then, I was very self-serving, and attempted to maneuver through certain situations in such a way as to benefit myself the most. Not saying I didn't care for anyone else to gain anything, but I was *always* looking to come out with something. But seeing my helpless, flailing, newborn child, I wanted to give him the world. I then discovered what it was to serve something, a bigger purpose, whether I got anything out of it or not. I am human, and bouts of selfishness continue even until now; but *discovering* that part of myself opened me up to a new realm of being. Now my wife, on the other hand, is the most unselfish person I know. But anyway... we're not talking about her.

Somehow, purpose will be *introduced* to you, just as it was to me the day my son came into the world. It will basically walk up and shake your hand, ask you a question, whisper in your ear. It will wake you up to a part of you that has seemed to be asleep, or it will awaken a desire to obtain all the tools you need to stand in it. If we are so overly introspective that we don't recognize it, we will continue to wander until we wake up one day in a place we truly despise. Because I was always controlled by circumstances and others' opinions, I'd wind up in that place consistently. There came a moment however, when I discovered that I *did* matter, that perhaps my purpose was greater than what nouns (people, places, and things-- see what I did there?) might grasp or even want me to think. That moment caused me to ask, *"What does this mean for me? what does this mean for others? how will this affect a bigger picture? is this so much bigger than me that I'm willing to lose something for it?"* When new opportunities arise for purpose and identity to be revealed in different ways, I try not to shy away from them. The more I welcome it, the more I perceive it when it knocks at my door.

Not all of us have been fortunate enough to have people in our lives that affirm us and encourage us in our own identity. Not having that is one of the main things that contributes to the capturing of our voice. However, as you'll read later, there comes a point where we need to "wake up" and decide for ourselves that *we become what we choose to become.* It's no one else's fault, now that you are able to make your own decisions. If you are a prisoner in this, remember that you are choosing to be a prisoner. *You do have a choice.* As painful as it may become, PUSH HARD against despair, PUSH HARD against whatever is oppressing and imprisoning you, PUSH HARD to reach the light of purpose.

Once we allow our purpose to help define our identity, and our identity define our purpose, our voice seems to become "unlocked." Because we have an increasing sureness of who we are, the things that combat our true voice don't seem so impossible to overcome. I have found this in my own life and have witnessed it in others'. When things come to shut me down or get me to unduly conform, I respond from a place of knowing my purpose. I am more equipped to answer the "what ifs" with a leap of faith when I know who I am. And when I know it's bigger than me, nothing can stop me.

Chapter 6
THE PEACE YOU THOUGHT WAS REAL

I felt it important to interject this short chapter, because before we can attempt to be healed from the things that ail us, we must be willing to see that something isn't right. You've likely heard this saying many times, that "*the first step in solving any problem is recognizing there is one.*" And so it is true with anything that is keeping us from becoming a more complete version of ourselves. I can ascertain with near 100% surety that you're reading this book because you realize that there is a problem somewhere. Kudos to you for taking that first step; now let's see if we're willing to take a few more steps.

In the "Grief and Trauma" chapter, we read about Maya Angelou's finding comfort in being silent. It was a kind of safe place for her, using *selective mutism* to hide away from any responsibility of facing a problem head on. It had become a pattern in her life, an accepted part of who she was, until she began to see it for what it was-- a crutch, a hindrance to growth, a slow death. Ms. Angelou had to actively refuse to revert to her coping mechanisms so that she could become something different. Many of us want to do better. We want to see ourselves become something greater than what life appears to have held us to. We want to experience an inner freedom that seems to consistently elude us. But are we willing to do the work to achieve it?

This next part may not sting at first, but as you ponder the question and read on, you may start to feel a bit uncomfortable. That's a good thing. But it's what you do afterwards that will matter most. My hope is that this book helps you walk this path to finding your voice with a real "light at the end of the tunnel" in view. Freedom is a reality, and my hope is that you walk through that door and don't look back. So, here's the question:

What are you doing to hold yourself back?

See? That didn't sting too badly.

I'd like to tell a little story. When my brothers and I were children, we'd visit my grandmother's house for holidays. My uncle, who at the time of my writing this is now a retired physician, would tell us to give him all our money. Although the situation was a lighthearted one, to my little mind, it felt like he was trying to take something away from me. The few pennies or nickels I had in my pocket were precious to me. It was mine. That's what made it precious– it belonged to me, so leave it alone. My younger brother, however, was a lot braver. He'd dig his little hands in his little pocket and offer my uncle the few cents he had. Then something happened that I didn't expect at first. My uncle took my brother's money, reached in his own pocket, then exchanged with him a handful of quarters and nickels and dimes; considerably more than my brother gave him.

Every time my uncle hears me tell this story, he gives me $100; so prayerfully he's reading this now. Over and over and over.

On a serious note, what strikes me about this story is that I don't recall feeling like I missed out on a great exchange. I don't remember feeling that perhaps I should have been less willing to hold on to my pennies so I could receive so much more. There was a lesson in what my uncle was doing, but I was content to keep my few cents– just don't touch what's mine.

A great many of us love the idea of becoming better versions of ourselves, but as soon as the part of our psyche that we deem "ours and ours alone" is addressed, we start to close ourselves off to what would probably benefit us. It's the part of us that has become a kind of "security blanket." We cry for help, but when the help comes in a way that makes us uncomfortable, we shut the door on it. It's like a patient visiting the doctor about headaches, and the doctor tells that patient to stop eating sugar so they can get to the root of a health issue– but the sweets-addicted patient says, "Can we just address what I came here for?" So I ask again:

What are you doing to hold yourself back?

We'll talk a bit later in the book about grape vines and their process, but did you know that literally ninety percent of a vine's growth is pruned every season? To the naked eye, it almost seems counterproductive. But as the season progresses, you begin to see the benefits of the pruning. The pruned vine is unrecognizable in only a few months because it has flourished beyond what our logical mind would have expected. But we neglect that process in its totality because we think– in our feeble minds– that we're good the way we are. If you were good the way you are, you'd have found your voice by now. But we've constructed an entire edifice around our false safe space and refuse to let it be addressed. We can perhaps talk about other sensitive issues we may have, but do not put a finger on *that thing*. It's our peace. It's our way of coping. It's how we stay strong.

It's not real.

What are you doing to hold yourself back?

We have accepted so many of these seemingly harmless-yet-harmful practices as "normal." We dismiss any suggestions that perhaps we need help by saying, "Leave it alone, that's just who I am." Let me be so bold to tell you that *it's not*. Think about it; why is that thing off limits?

If we are going to grow into a freer, fuller person, everything must be laid out– even the uncomfortable things. It doesn't have to be all at once, but eventually you'll need to decide if it's worth your life. Why was I ok with my few pennies when much more was available to me? I literally ask myself questions like these when I notice myself being comfortable with unhealthy patterns. When I do, I learn that:

1. Mistrust is not ok as a "jerk" reaction

2. An unproductive habit needs to either be adjusted or done away with

3. I need to choose to be uncomfortable for the sake of my and possible others' futures

4. I am not the only one who can help me

There is so much more I can add to this list, but the point is that we must recognize that sometimes, our peaceful, safe space is really just a mask that keeps us either practicing or hiding from the effects of trauma. Essentially, they're one and the same. Let's open up a little. You're safe. Remember, your voice *wants* to be free. It's yearning for the _actual_ reality of what it's supposed to be, not the false one that's been set up around it. You are the steward of it, so don't rob yourself or anyone else of the gift that you are.

Don't hold yourself back anymore.

Chapter 7
FINDING YOUR VOICE: THE
MASK COMES OFF

I started out singing around the piano with my mother and brothers at a very young age. She would show us the basics of piano and teach us songs; then in the summertime we'd sing in front of my grandmother's church. As I got older, music remained a huge part of my identity, even as I acquired other skills and nurtured other gifts. I didn't get truly serious as a vocalist until I was seventeen years old.

At that age, I fell in love with the voice of singer Brian McKnight, and if you've ever heard him, you know why. Seeing as he was the best vocalist at the time in my opinion, I began to mimic the things that he'd do with his voice, the fluctuations, the runs, the style. I also loved the voice of another singer whose music my mother had introduced me to, Will Downing. Whenever I'd sing a Will Downing song, I'd imitate Will's voice; and likewise with a Brian McKnight song, I'd imitate Brian. My mother heard me sing one of Will Downing's songs at a school talent show, and being a mother, she was in tears because of my performance. Some time later, however,

she expressed to me that although I had sung the song beautifully, it sounded to her like I was "holding back."

Being the teenager that I was, I was a bit offended that she would say that. I mean, I was doing my darnedest to sound the best I could. Everyone had told me that it was the most beautiful performance of the night. The high school choir director had told me he thought my voice was gorgeous. I even gained female admirers because of my awesome singing. How DARE my mother dampen things by telling me that I wasn't as superb as I thought I was? Holding back?? Thanks for the encouragement, MOTHER.

But what my mother was saying was not that I didn't sound good or do well; she wasn't even saying that I wasn't the best that night. She was saying, "Yes, you did Will Downing well, but I want to hear your *own* voice come out from behind that." I must say that at that time, I knew *exactly* what she meant. I just wasn't expecting anyone besides myself to notice that I was hiding behind my favorite singers' voices. But I knew all the voices that everyone loved, and I wanted to sound like them. I was afraid that my own natural voice would be inadequate; therefore, I didn't bother to explore it.

It's something I see so often, and since I am a father with the *heart of* a father, it's easy to discern when people are exuding a persona other than their own. It's like there is something making that person believe that who they are behind the facade is less than acceptable. And I have learned that it doesn't necessarily require someone else to defame or criticize that person to cause this insecurity; it can simply be that they want to be as successful or popular or awesome as whoever it is they are imitating. Sometimes it can be that he or she received little or no affirmation in his or her own personality or ability. To gain acceptance, they "move with the tide", or even change like a chameleon if they think that's what will do the trick. Listen to me– I'm not talking about children and peer pressure, I'm talking about adults who have practiced this behavior for so long that many times they, themselves, believe their own front. I once heard Leann Squier, a fellow singer, say (paraphrased), "Wherever you're really supposed to be, people will love you." In other words, if you are in the space you were created to occupy, with the people (be it friends, coworkers, constituents, students, whatever) you were made to be around, doing the thing you were created to do, you won't have to worry about whether or not you are received as who you really are. Your God-given gift will fit. Your voice will be heard.

One of the problems is, again, we have no clue of the value of our own voice. In my line of work, sometimes it is difficult to get people to recognize that although they may not have a singing voice like mine or Whitney Houston's (see what I did there?), that is by no means a measuring stick for whether their voice is worth listening to. So they either shut down completely, or try to shape themselves into something acceptable. But let's look at someone like the British singer, Dido. She thought she was just a "shower singer" until someone who loved her voice felt she could have a following. When we hear Dido sing, we know it's her; her voice is unique; and from what I can tell, she didn't change her singing to fit some vocal status quo. Think of some of the great music we could be missing out on if some of those we'd typically have considered "less talented" would have remained silent. We can relate this to so many areas other than music; some people's unique voice is in their art, others' can be in their skills, or in the way they speak publicly, for example.

The key is recognizing that *everything has some value.*

We are made up of many things, tangible and intangible. We know that we have skin, limbs, muscles, organs. We have a brain where every memory is stored, a nervous system that causes us to sense and feel physical touch. But we are also made up of the sum of our thoughts, our patterns, our emotions and desires. As we discussed earlier, things happen– good or bad– that affect that intangible part of us, which invariably affects our expression. That is 100% true, whether we recognize it or not. It's the reason for things like depression (whether caused by chemical imbalance or not), PTSD, and diabetes. OK, not diabetes; that's just a test to see if you're paying attention. Without learning the value in our vocal expression, we tend to fall into and linger in the negative effects of life issues. Anger, violence, addictions, all materialize and have roots in misplaced emotions that have no idea how to find their way out as a "pure" stream. Things will happen. Bad things will happen. But what avenue are we affording ourselves to allow a positive freedom of expression?

It is very difficult to climb out of the black hole of silence without an avenue to release your voice. I found myself feeling very trapped in a void-like state, if you will, trying to figure out who I was, even after being married, having children, entering the career I'd always wanted, and getting to experience the great places I'd never imagined I'd experience. So how did I get on the road to finding that avenue?

I'm glad you asked.

I don't know how "life messages" are conveyed to you, the reader, in your season-byseason life, but I dream often. Many times those dreams speak to the deep part of me and address life issues that need addressing. Some years ago, I dreamt that I was sitting at a table, looking through some old drawings I had done when I was younger. (I used to be a very good artist.) As I went through them, I said under my breath, "Man, what happened to me; I used to be so good." I heard a voice behind me respond. I don't remember what the voice said, but I knew it was in response to me. Knowing I wasn't speaking loud enough for anyone to hear me, I was intrigued to know how anyone could respond as if I was speaking out loud. So I decided to test it once more.

I said, even more quietly, "Man, I used to be so good." The voice behind me responded.

"Well, you still can be." Now I knew without a doubt that the voice was answering me.

I had to know who this was and how she was doing that. I walked over and said, "Hey, that is so cool... How do you do that?" Before she could answer, I saw that it was the late American comedian, Joan Rivers. She had passed already, and I knew this in the dream; so I knew this was a divine appointment. I introduced myself. "Wow, you're Joan Rivers! I'm James Vincent."

"Oh, we know you," she said, indicating that the people in heaven knew who I was. "Your name is in the board."

I was so pleased to know this. But then she continued.

"By your name it says, 'Could have been the Great of God, but wanted to look good.'" That cut me to my heart. I began to weep, because nothing means more to me than pleasing the God that I serve, and being all that I'm created to be in that. "Well geez," she said as I wept, "It's not like it's too late... You can still change..." Then I awoke.

Wow. That spoke to me and caused me to ponder my life. I realized that in the midst of all I was doing, in every effort to go farther than I'd ever been and excel in what I do, there was still a huge part of me that was wearing a mask in order to please people. I wasn't allowing the intrinsic gifts to manifest to the fullest because I was trying to fit in someone else's world by suppressing pieces of my being. I couldn't blame anyone but myself.

No one on this earth– no matter what anyone says to you– owns your soul but you; that is, unless you give it away. If you feel oppressed by someone or something, know that you have a choice whether or not you will remain oppressed. Like I mentioned before, let the "what ifs" work themselves out; but know whatever the cause of the suppression of your voice, it's your choice to either stay there or to get on a better road to freedom. I chose to get on that road to freedom, and although it's been rocky at times, I rest in knowing that the alternative is to leave this life still trying to "look good" for other people.

Either way, no one has to answer for me but me; that's the point of me telling this dream. Any mask we wear is a mask we bear the responsibility for either keeping up or destroying.

My mother was wanting to draw something hidden out of me when she "called me out" about holding back. She didn't want to hear Will Downing or Brian McKnight when I sang, she wanted to hear her son's voice come out from behind that. I became freer and freer in my expression after being confronted by that dream (and other challenges), and also decided not to suppress any other gifts on the inside; to explore all those things I was so afraid to allow room for inside the world in which I lived. Read this excerpt I found on a page of www.stemmenbakstemmen.no, by Beate Myrvold, a voice teacher in Oslo, Norway, that had to do with vocal training and some of the psychology behind exploring the voice:

One of my greatest inspirators mentioned before, Alfred Wolfson, put it like this: "If you can't sing the evil, the evil will sing you", - meaning that if you don't dare to work with all the different levels when working with the voice, truly there will be something that interfere with the "free voice", - or a technically good balanced voice, or the ability to express something genuine.

We cannot come around or bypass the fact that previous negative experiences shape and influence the voice in one way or another, whether that may be physical "uncontrolled constrictions", low self-esteem, lack of authenticity or ability to experiment.

In an earlier part of the article that I didn't include here, the writer started with the notion that we are born already instinctively using all of the vocal mechanics needed to produce to clearest, purest, loudest sound. But somewhere along the way, we began to lose that instinct, and became afraid to explore it when the time came to address the issues. But we don't seem to want to choose, as the writer put it, that "genuine" part of us, because we are afraid of what we'll find. Hopefully you've read the previous chapters, because this next statement won't make sense unless you have:

Go jump off a cliff.

Again, it is a conscious choice people like us have to make, because if not, we will look in the mirror a decade from now and see the same confined, quiet, confused, angry person we've been since we lost our true voice. Don't– I repeat– DO NOT try to understand this process in its entirety. One of the things I encounter most with those I've helped is that they want all the answers *right now*, and since the way is a bit cloudy or solutions are somewhat elusive, they remain stuck.

Can you do yourself a favor? OK, do it for me. Close this book right now and do something you've never done that represents your letting go and leaving the confines of whatever is keeping you bound up. Scream out of the window. Tap dance on your car. Wear white after Labor Day*! Give that mean neighbor a hug. Tell your boss, *"You can't fire me... I QUIT!!!"* OK, you may want to reconsider that last one, but whatever you decide to do and however you do it, close this book right now and take off the mask.

---

*Labor Day is an American holiday, after which the fashion custom is that one should not wear white until late spring/early summer.

Chapter 8

FINDING YOUR VOICE: THE BIG SQUEEZE

Well, I certainly hope you took some time to do something liberating to your inner self. If not, I'll assume you're reading this on a airplane, in a library, or in a public restroom stall.

I said in the previous chapter that there is a conscious choice we need to make to get on a clear path to realizing our true voice. I am a firm believer in not having to individually address every negative issue before becoming a better person; just choose to be better and start taking steps in that direction. That's one mistake I see often when I'm dealing with people-- they want to be perfect *before* they move forward. This fosters a continual attitude of inadequacy, and even if that person feels they've attained some form of adequacy (in one's own mind), it only proves to be a huge setup for major failure. Trust me, as long as there is breath in our bodies, there will be opportunity to deal with issues that need attention. And we don't want to find ourselves stagnate just because things around us don't seem to be changing.

Along with this choice comes the bittersweet inevitable: things will happen in our lives whose sole purpose is to sharpen us and squeeze out our full expression. It's a journey. We are hopefully constantly discovering ourselves until the day we die; the goal is to be free enough and aware enough to stay on that journey. Who are you today? Are you open to being shaped into someone new tomorrow?

For a few years, I took on a viticulturist job, as part of my background is gardening and landscaping. Taking care of and cultivating grapevines is an exquisitely different experience than other aspects of gardening, especially when these grapes are being grown for wine making. In that season, I had to learn new things, think differently, experiment in ways I had never experimented, and above all, *learn patience.* I started that vineyard pretty much from the ground up. When you know that by conventional methods a vineyard doesn't produce wine worth selling until about its fifth year, you have got to begin with some patience. But patience in and of itself isn't what I'm focusing on- there are books about that. I'm focusing on the process of growing, cultivating, and producing from grapevines, and how that relates to this topic of your voice getting free.

By no means do I consider myself an expert in viticulture; if anything, I'm still kind of a student. However, many of the things I learned while caring for these vines have stayed with me, and I have often implemented many of these lessons in areas of my own life. There is the process of being planted. After the soil is prepared, either a vine or cutting from a vine is placed in the ground. As we all know, water, the right amount of sun and shade, and climate all affect the well being of a plant, especially a new plant. As the vine grows, care must be given to train the shoots along the trellis in such a way where there is a picture of what we want to vine to look like in the future. It is nowhere near ready to produce wine-making grapes, but the time to begin to take shape for this is now. Most wine grape growers will remove any grape flowers (which turn into grape clusters) in order to allow it to focus on establishing a healthy root system and trunk.

Sometimes, the reason we have a hard time knowing and/or expressing the truth of who we are is the fact that we are not willing to fully immerse ourselves in the process it takes to reach maturity. Don't ask me why (since I don't know why myself), but I seem to have some special gift of staying in the process. Here's the thing– I don't ever remember *enjoying* the process. Many times I have found myself thinking I'm ready to "produce grapes", only to find that the process will only take longer. Something in me, that I can only attribute to something greater than I, would keep me from abandoning the process and continue to have my clusters picked off as my roots were established. This is extremely uncomfortable, but extremely important to realizing potential. Have you found yourself looking back at your life and seeing that if you would have stayed in a particular process, you would have added value to your potential? Whether you are 20, 40, 60, or even 85, as long as there is breath in your body, it's not too late to produce a "fine wine" of your life.

The process I'm talking about isn't one that always presents itself in obvious form. By that, I mean there are processes we all enter, like school, internships, dating, child-rearing, etc. But then there are other things that happen that are more like "curve balls" thrown into our lives; things that are likely meant to stretch and sharpen us to a point that we come out with hope and resilience we didn't know we were capable of. Although these things are meant to make us better and shape us to add to our value and potential, too many times we succumb to the oppressing power of a thing, and never subdue it with the power waiting to be unlocked inside of us. I touched on this in the chapter about grief and trauma; that we allow ourselves to be reduced instead of increased. Much like grape pruning, everything that is cut away is so that we can come out with much more than we began with. With proper pruning techniques, the vine grows in such a way that when it is allowed to produce, the grape clusters are plentiful and uniform.

The methods used for cultivating wine grapes are not only to produce *lots* of berries– they are to produce grapes that possess the right amount of water, sugar, and *character* to create a unique, viable, and enjoyable product. I so love the parallelism between grapevines and people! When I tell you that my time in the vineyard was spent learning about myself, I'm not just saying that for effect, or to legitimize the topic of this book, I literally stood in amazement at how everything the grapes had to go through to reach its fullest potential so related to the human experience. Below is one of the best ways I've seen it explained by UK based wine journalist, Jamie Goode, on his online magazine dedicated to all things wine, www.wineanor ak.com:

More modern methods of growing grapes, in close-spaced rows on wire trellising, take advantage of the fact that <u>making the vines struggle</u> generally results in better quality grapes. It's a bit like people. Place someone in a nearperfect environment, giving them every comfort and all that they could ever want to satisfy their physical needs, and it could have rather disastrous consequences for their personality and physique. If you take a grapevine and make its physical requirements for water and nutrients easily accessible, then (somewhat counterintuitively) it will give you poor grapes.

Forgive my anthropomorphism, but this is   because the grapevine has a choice. Given a favourable environment and it will choose to take the vegetative route: that is, it will put its energies into making leaves and shoots. Effectively, it is saying, 'This is a fine spot, I'm going to make myself at home here'. It won't be too bothered about making grapes. But make things difficult for the vine, by restricting water supply, making nutrients scarce, pruning it hard and crowding it with close neighbours, and it will take the hump. It will sense that this is not the ideal place to be a grapevine. Instead of devoting itself to growing big and sprawling, it will focus its effort on reproducing itself sexually, which for a vine means making grapes.

In essence, I believe it's safe to say that we *need* life to be difficult in some instances so that we can realize who we really are and what we are capable of. We need whirlwinds to come and create a little havoc in order to produce the right amount of stress; giving us the right concentration of our own unique qualities that show the beauty of us. The main reason for growing grapevines is to produce grapes; and as the writer above said, if the vine is given an easy environment to flourish in, the grape production will be poor. It will have lots of pretty leaves with no decent fruit to offer. Have you been searching and fighting for ways to rid your life of every obstacle, for ways to experience a life devoid of the challenges that help to produce character? If so, then I can probably show you one of the reasons you're not on the path you need to be on in life. It's that path that helps us to find and develop the depth of our voice.

As I look back on my life, I can truly say that, one way or another, every stormy situation I've experienced has created some form of maturity in me and added something to my overall personality and relation to life in general. Every time I have a negative reaction to something because of past experience, I have to reassess, revisit, and confront whatever is causing my hostile attitudes. And I have to be willing to get real. Every time we get real about something and deal with it *head on*, we have created a new opportunity to step into that much more freedom. (see the chapter, *"The Peace You thought was Real"*)

For the longest time, there were things I would not say about my childhood because I didn't want to make anyone look bad. And while my upbringing wasn't nearly as wretched as some, it wasn't without its "taboo-ness". (Yep, I just coined that word. *"Taboo-niciosity"*, maybe?) I won't go into great detail here, but my siblings and I went through some things that not every child experiences, although I wouldn't consider our story unique. Now, in all, I had a decent upbringing. For much of my life, I was raised in a Christian home, went to decent schools, was regularly fed, had certain privileges, etc. My parents cared about our general well being; I was never without basic necessities. However, throughout my youth, there was always an afflicting atmosphere of something awful, something that seemed to greatly subtract from an enjoyable childhood experience. Being a child of divorced parents, and then suddenly part of a new, blended family was already a lot for a young child to juggle through; but then to live with all the other more specific issues that came along with it amounted to years of longing, tears, excruciatingly agonizing fears, and heartache. About six years into my marriage, I finally felt like I released some of the pent-up emotion that resulted from those years of my upbringing. I remember it so clearly; I was getting ready to run a 5k race for the first time, and as I prepared that morning, something came over me. I don't recall what brought on the discussion of my childhood, but I fell to my knees and began to weep. "I *hated* my childhood!" I sobbed. It was my first time coming to grips with– and *voicing*– that notion. I had never even hinted to anyone about that deep thing that steeped in the recesses of my soul for all those years. I'd so wanted to protect my parents' and my image that I'm not so sure I was aware how much I hated my childhood. Something was released that morning; a part of me was unlocked. There were areas of maturation in my life that I couldn't fully enter into without acknowledging that part of myself, so I needed to face those demons in order to grow more effectively and fruitfully. No one is perfect. No parent is perfect. I am a parent and I recognize that we rarely get it right. But everything we encounter– past, present, and future– is all part of the process. It's what adds to our identity.

I ran a pretty good 5k that day, too.

How many of us have deep regrets in our lives that, if we had the power, we would reverse whatever brought on that regret? I've fallen into that category many times. But, as we all no doubt have heard at one time or another, we learn from those things. Take a moment to ask yourself what you gained from those things you wish never would have happened. I guarantee that in the least, you know which way *not* to go, or what *to* do in the future. When we don't take time to healthily reflect on these things, but allow it to fester into something horrible (see the chapter on grief and trauma), we develop a huge wall, a *silence* if you will, that stops us from moving into the next phase of who we are.

When I worked in the vineyard, I was required to grow and cultivate the vines organically. I am already what many would consider a "purist" when it comes to certain things, so it was not a huge leap for me to immerse myself within this concept. As I discovered the parallels between vine care and the human experience, I thought to myself, *"Hmm... if we, who are alive, are made to recover from certain diseases and ailments, then I could ascertain that*

91

plant life has the same intrinsic ability." So, where most growers, even organic growers, would resort to using chemical methods to treat aggressive diseases, I would do my best to create an environment that would allow the plant to heal on its own. What many of us don't realize is that a plant is not necessarily the sum of what we see above ground. By that, I mean that many plants, if they are pruned, cut down, or affected by disease to the point that they lose fruit and foliage, there is still a "nurturable" element of life that exists somewhere within it. I have seen the grapevines affected so badly that I thought they were totally dead. But before I proceeded to dig them up, I noticed something amazing... there were little sprouts just above the ground, showing signs of life from the plants I thought would not recover. So that's when I resolved to give every vine a chance to overcome every insect, disease, and climate issue by promoting an environment that would pull forth its own "desire" to heal. Many times, the vines came back stronger and more prolific than before!

Again, I'm not an expert on viticulture, I'm just relating my experiences. I'm sure for those whose livelihood is growing organic grapes, sometimes conventional methods are necessary in extreme situations. For the sake of finding your voice, however, we need to understand the resilient core of life that resides within us. Too many times, we are willing to be "dug up" instead of giving ourselves a chance to bounce back with vigor and hope. *It is in you.*

I and my wife recently met with a young lady whom we consider a daughter. She was at the point of distress and despair because she felt like she wasn't where she wanted to be in life, and the place where she was at the time was not conducive to the dreams she had for herself. At the same time, she wanted to be sure that she wasn't being so ambitious to the point that she would cause a disaster in her own life for the sake of chasing a dream. She is a very talented singer and musician, and I could immediately relate to her grievance from that standpoint. We knew that she was at a point in her life that she was being squeezed. It's that point where you are being so tested and feel so much circumstantial pressure that you want to jump out of the process to free yourself from the chaos. I agree - that would feel so good. *So* good. But we told her to take a look at where she had come from, look at where she is now, and believe that there is a path into her future. Sometimes we think we know what our future should be, simply because we know what we want. That's not always the case; in fact, it's rarely the case. Go have a conversation with the average person who attained what he/she *thought* they wanted. You'll find that there is usually something missed or overlooked, some process they wish they could go back and better walk through. Believe me, your voice comes alive as you follow the road that was meant for you to travel.

We also told this young lady to remember that she is the only one has to answer for her own decisions in the end. Many times we take that as some sort of heavy admonition about consequences, but what we were attempting to get through to her was that when all is said and done, her life is no one else's but *hers* and *God's*. So she had to be careful of being overrun by others' voices, and being pulled into doing things in such a way that the truth of who she is would be compromised. Take good advice, but don't be controlled. And remember that sometimes, just sometimes, someone else is wiser than you.

Like we read earlier in the excerpt about the vines, if they were left solely to their own devices, they would grow, grow, grow, spread, spread, spread, but produce little or poor fruit. They require someone to come in and "teach" the vines to be productive by facilitating the right nourishment, hacking away at it, giving and taking as needed, and even creating an "uncomfortable" environment for it. We told this young lady not to walk through this time of her life alone; that we were committed to seeing her through this uneasy time of squeezing. It's the squeezing that gets the good juice out of the grapes to make wine, but it's everything else that leads up to the squeezing that gives the wine its character. Could it be that we don't fully know our voice yet? Could it be, perhaps, that before our voice can truly be heard, sometimes there is more we have to mature through? Know the voices you can trust to help you make it through the maturing process. And remember that no matter your age, there will always be *some* maturing to do. Wine made from a mature five year-old vine will have different characteristics from wine made from that same vine at fifteen years.

It's no wonder we hear some singers and performers singing songs and playing parts whose voices we have a hard time believing. It's like hearing a ten-year-old sing about falling in love and having babies. Something about that just isn't quite as honest as when it comes from someone who has truly experienced falling in love. Mature vines naturally make the most complex wine. Likewise, voices that have been allowed to mature through its natural, unique process convey the most honest message and sound. Answer this question for yourself: *do you want your unique voice to be heard, or do you want to repeat someone else's sound?* That's what will happen if you don't allow yourself to continue in the journey specifically fashioned for you.

Here We Go 'Round the Mountain

Let's say, for example, a grapevine wanted to make good wine, so it tried and tried, but nothing around it changed. When a viticulturist came to help it out and help shape it into the best producer it could be, it turned its nose up at her and said, "I'm a grapevine, THANK you... I got this." The viticulturist says, "I know you're a grapevine. I'm not trying to turn you into something else, I only want to give you the tools to be the best *you* that you can be."

The vine says, "Oh, but I already make grapes."

The viticulturist says, "Yeah, I know... But there is so much more to you than that. Please, just let me walk with you through the process, and I will do everything in my power to see to it that you make the most unique wine. Just ask your buddies, Chardonnay and Cabernet; it wasn't the most painless journey, but now they produce some awesome wine."

"Thanks, but no thanks," says the vine. "There's got to be an easier way than that."

This is how so many of us remain where we are; in a cycle that we basically see we need to break, but we don't want the difficulty that comes along with coming out of the cycle. Much like the story in the bible where Moses led the whining and ungrateful group of Israelites out of Egypt, we go around and around the same mountain because we don't want to submit to and learn from everything that is presented on our path, good or bad. A challenge is presented, and we shrink back from it; yet we want all the benefits that come from overcoming that challenge! There is only one way to benefit from overcoming a challenge... OVERCOME THE CHALLENGE! Face it, and decide that your future– even someone *else's* future– is worth it.

During the season that I worked in the vineyard, there were other things that I helped to oversee. One of those things was landscape maintenance, which we had hired out to another company; it was a very big job. One of the guys on our staff suggested to my boss that we transfer the task of landscape maintenance to the in-house crew. I was totally against the idea. I didn't want to be part of cutting grass and lawn labor. I felt like that period of my life had passed; it was personally time to move on to better things. To my dismay, my boss accepted his proposal.

Several years prior, I'd worked a night job in a refrigeration warehouse that supplied a chain of grocery stores. It wasn't the best line of work, but I supported my family for the better part of about five years there. There was a particular task there that everyone unanimously agreed was the toughest job on site– preparing egg orders, or "egg throwing", as it was wittily nicknamed. One person would be chosen as the egg thrower if he was good at his job in other areas, ironically, as a reward; it was a type of promotion. When the "reigning eggman" left the company, *yours truly* (that's me) was awarded the ever-so-envied spot.

I hated that job. My wife, my pastor, even many of my coworkers knew that I was not at all fond of this position. But somewhere along the way, I settled within myself that complaining and having a bad attitude would not help me in any way, especially since it didn't seem like I was going anywhere else any time soon. I learned in that period of my life that I was fully capable of enduring trying situations that, in the end, may prove beneficial to my growth. I worked that particular position until the company shut down and relocated to another city.

So there I was, nearly ten years later, faced with another task that I'd long dreaded being thrust upon me. Although the guy who'd made the proposal was one of my close friends, that day he most certainly wasn't. I moped through the next few work days, wondering which job would be mine; mowing, trimming, edging, thinking how funky life must be to once again put me in this position. Then it hit me.

I've been here before.

"Did I learn *nothing* from the 'egg throwing' experience?" I had to ask myself. In that moment I quickly decided that I was not going to complain, and since I had maneuvered well through a similar situation in times past, I could do it again. I decided that I would be content within myself and let nothing dictate my emotional state. No sooner had I resolved my grievances, when my boss approached me with: "Yeah, James... They're taking over the grass cutting, but I don't want you to have to do all that. Let the others handle it." I must say that my elated, approving grin was difficult to hide.

That moment would have been much less gratifying had I not accepted what life was giving me and decided to master it, and not let it master me. I didn't allow my life lessons to go to waste, but I pulled what I gained from one adverse situation to help me work through another; and in the end it benefited me more than I knew it would– much like the grapevine.

Because of this and many other (more difficult) situations like it, I have substance behind my words when I encourage people to learn from life- not to try to escape it or work around it. Our approach to life generally determines how our voice is shaped in the end. If you have not done it yet, take some time to examine your life; reflect and see what journey you've been on until now. What have you gained? Don't just look at what you've learned– like you learned how to spell c-a-t in school– but look at what has been added to you. Then answer the following questions.

What challenges have you faced that have given you a voice for this moment in your life?

Is what you've learned helping you at this point on your path?

What parts of your journey are difficult to revisit?

Are you willing to confront your past and let it benefit you, or let it keep control of a portion of your voice?

How are you being stretched and squeezed now? or are you somehow avoiding a new maturing process in your life?

Chapter 9
REGAINING YOUR VOICE:
BREAK FREE

The voice is an extremely powerful tool. As previously stated, the voice is not limited to the movement of breath and the vibration of vocal cords. There is profound power in bodily communication, in our actions and deeds, the manner in which we impact the general public, and the list goes on. Your voice is essentially an extension of your *self.* When we discover that we actually have something unique to contribute, the realm of possibility expands for us; it's like we enter into an entirely new world of freedom, expression, and power. I can honestly say that for me, it was an entirely new beginning in my life.

Get mad

As a young singer in a Christian worship setting, I remember being extremely conscious of everyone's opinion of me. I wanted to be well-thought of; to have nothing less than stellar things said about me. Because we are taught not to seek our own glory, I would intentionally mask my true skills as a singer. I'd hold back from really "letting loose" when singing songs because I didn't want anyone to think I was showing off my skills for the sake of wowing the crowd. Although no one had ever directly put that pressure on me, my fear of people's opinion caused me to suppress myself in order to appear to be a "good Christian."

I'm going to assume here that most reading this book are familiar with the story of Jesus Christ's birth, death, and resurrection– if not, you can find it in the first four books in the New Testament of the bible. But one day as I was getting ready to minister in song, still being guided by my own fear-laced boundaries, I looked out at the audience. It was as if the room darkened, the spotlight shone on me, and suddenly no one else was there. At once, the liberating truth became more of a reality than I'd ever realized:

Not one of these people out here died for me.

It was that moment that made me most aware of the fact that in the end, I didn't owe any man anything concerning what I was created to do and be.

For me, God was the only one I owed my life to because of His willingness to give up His only son, Jesus Christ, so that I could become free of the things that held me like a prisoner and live life to the fullest. I began to sing my heart out without holding back, because I was no longer singing with a people-consciousness, but I was singing for God alone. If people hated me for it (and I've had bad things said about me), that was literally their own problem in my mind, because I wasn't pouring my being out for them anyway.

Subsequently, many more pieces of myself seemed to become unlocked little by little. It truly was a very real moment for me. And there are yet still things I'm discovering about myself; things I'd lost and am now rediscovering, as well as things I'd never explored. What realization have you come to– or feel you should come to– in your life that could help you uncover pieces to whom you really are?

I must admit that I was somewhat evasive a moment ago, when I simply said that pieces of myself seemed to become unlocked little by little; I left something out, and I'd like to give the fullest picture possible. During that fresh start in that season of my life, I was continually reminded, as new situations would arise, of how much control of my life I had given to others; whether they were bosses, relatives, church leaders, bad habits, whatever. It was like I was looking at a near-empty canvas of a supposed life painting, that should have been full of vibrant colors and varying themes. It was like a garden full of dirt and rocks with no fruit to show for whatever seeds had been planted.

I got mad.

I decided in that season that no matter how nervous I'd get, or how much anything or anyone would attempt to overwhelm me with floods of discouragement, I was not going to be silenced any longer. It angered me to discover how much farther along I could have been in life, had I not been so timid and self-conscious. I couldn't blame anyone except myself for all the wasted years of overly caring about what people thought of me, of all the time spent trying to figure out how *not* to create a stir. Sure, there were things that had occurred in my life that I could point to in order to analyze how and why I got to the obscure place where I'd found myself; but in the end, my choices and fears were just that– *mine.*

I understand that many circumstances are beyond our control, that in some instances we were blind-sided by unlikely events. But am I still allowing myself to be dictated to by everything that has happened to me up until now?

Some of us are not willing to take responsibility for our position in life. Sometimes, taking responsibility is all we need to see ourselves a bit more clearly. The less we want to open our eyes to what's really happening within ourselves– and I mean *deep* within ourselves– the more likely we are to remain in a space we were not meant to occupy. I could have convinced myself that if someone would've just given me a chance, they'd see the amazing person I'm truly capable of being. But then, I'd be fostering an attitude that will *always* wait around for someone else to let me be who I am. And I'd still essentially be going nowhere.

Once we decide to take responsibility for our own lives, we discover the power we truly have to break free. As we discussed in the previous chapter, it's a process, but our willingness to enter into and master the process is a victory in itself!

I tell this story because I believe our voice needs to have a solid, unshakable reason to come alive and *stay* alive. For me, I have a decreasing desire to please people, and a greatly increasing desire to serve God with all I am; and in turn lead others to that same freedom. For others, perhaps they can't stand by any longer and watch injustices go uncontested, or maybe some have discovered their ability to be a mouthpiece for those without a voice. Whatever it is, it's got to go far beyond ourselves and some fleeting desire to make a noise that gives us a meaningless spotlight. Or else, after so long, you'll find yourself consistently back at square one, feeling you've accomplished nothing and still have no idea who you are really meant to be.

Have you ever noticed how some people filter everything through their insecurities, negative outlook on life, or other less-than-kosher attitudes and habits? I've seen it– the overweight woman, the victim of racism, the scorned lover– all masks that have had power handed to them; masks designed to wreak havoc on people's souls. Their voices bleed with the inimical effects of these ravagers (discussed in the "Voice Raiders" chapters). What we are looking for is a way to harness the power that frees us from these effects. We can read books like the one you're reading now, we can go to seminars, even take pills... But the power needs to become a *reality* to us. That reality is what caused me to get mad. It's what causes many to come out from oblivion and make themselves useful to society. If it's not real, it will remain a fantasy in our minds, as if we are attempting to control the wind– we can try, but deep on the inside, we know it's impossible.

Listen!

One of the more pressing issues when discovering our voice is *learning how* to express whatever it is we want to convey. What does this have to do with breaking free? Because it's one thing to "feel the power" and get a sudden zing of zeal; it's another thing to be able to effectively use the awesome tool you've been given in your voice. "Breaking free" includes cutting off whatever is rendering your voice powerless and learning how to properly use it; and "properly" means different things for different people, as each voice is unique.

I have found that the most useful tool in gaining effectiveness in the voice is... are you ready for it? *Listening.* I don't think we realize the power that lies in simply listening. We've already touched on the fact that we must realize that our voice is not the only voice that matters, that we don't have all the answers, and that we need to know when to be silent and when to exert ourselves. Effective listening is not only useful, it's *empowering.* How do I know? Because for the longest time, I was the only one I'd listen to! My viewpoint was the only one that mattered to me. And since I was so introverted and (secretly) obstinate, my voice had no reason to break free. It was me against the world... so I just stayed in my world. But when I, through a series of life events and lessons, began to come out from beyond my stubborn walls and learn to listen– sincerely listen– a new realm of confidence in my own expression began to unfold.

OK, my wife wouldn't let me stay stubborn; so yeah... I was a bit forced to learn to listen. I'm still getting better; and my voice is still finding new ways and avenues of release. So here is a question for you: when was the last time you listened to someone, with the genuine intent to take in and process what he or she is expressing? I find that my children respond to my voice with much more reverence and appreciation when they feel that I listen to them with sincerity, for example. I do my best to *listen in detail*. I remind people of what they've said to me, I ask questions, and I let them know when I'm not understanding, or even not actually listening. I don't turn the conversation on myself unless I find that it can in some way help or add to the depth of what's been referenced. These are just examples of practices in learning to listen.

If you haven't tried this already, try it– your voice will thank you.

Vocalize!

I have had so many people tell me that they wish they could overcome their timidity in order to express themselves the way they'd like to. While it would be wonderful to give a five or ten-step process to getting past that obstacle, I've given everyone the same response: *you've just got to do it*. Again, we don't realize that although we may have been oppressed, suppressed, deceived, mocked, or whatever has contributed to keeping our voice on lock-down, we actually have all the tools we need to at least get on the road to breaking free. The first time I ever sang a solo in front of a crowd, I was frightened out of my mind! But the only way for me to overcome that fear was to step out and do it. There was no waiting for the fear to pass, no reading a book to find out how to climb that mountain. I had to decide that that was as good a moment as any to conquer that fear. Now, here I am years later, continually singing in front of thousands. And it pays the bills.

For many, it may be having to do things like saying "no" more, or saying "yes" more. Maybe it's speaking up at any cost, or something as simple as being the first to say, "Hello." It may even take a few times, but whatever it is, keep doing it until you believe it! If you never believe it, it will never last as part of your thought pattern– and we need our minds to comply with our newly discovered freedom. We are so afraid of being rejected that many times we don't step out when we could. Our downfall is that we internalize that rejection (or the *possibility of*) and let it take hold of our mental process instead of using it as fuel that continues to empower us. We can learn from all the adversity that comes our way. Again, it's all part of the process, and a changing thought pattern is vital to fashioning a lifestyle of liberty. Keep doing the useful things that your mind keeps telling you *not* to do, and it will eventually change.

I've heard stories of people simply becoming sick of doing nothing and feeling like their lives were going nowhere; so they got up and *did something*. They volunteered at a community center or nursing home. They wrote books. They joined a choir. Sometimes, it's not so much figuring out *why* your voice is shut down as it is getting out and doing something. Let me say that again.

Sometimes, it's not so much figuring out why *your voice is shut down as it is getting out and doing something.*

What's been there all along will begin to finally see the light of day, and perhaps one thing will lead to another as you find your true identity.

"Well, it's just not that simple," you may say. *"That's great for some people, but my demons are much greater than all this."* I understand that issues vary from person to person. Some things are more difficult to overcome than others. But the bottom line remains: how much do you really want to break free

and regain your true identity? Most of the time, our excuses don't do anything except reinforce our chains. I love the story an associate of mine, Joseph Pierce, told about a conversation between him and his wife as they discussed some heavy marital issues. It serves to say, before you read on, that this man had an extremely difficult upbringing, including having a mother who was a convicted murderer, he had a bad "rap sheet" in a boys home, was dishonorably discharged from the military, and the list goes on.

"Well you don't know what it was like for me as a child!" he whined.

"And I don't want to know!" retorted his wife.

It was in that season he discovered that his past problems should not be a recurring excuse for him not to grow in his marriage. His wife, although appearing insensitive on the surface (I'm not sure how I would have taken that!), was concerned about the here-and-now, how they could overcome and grow; not stew and shrivel. She was not concerned, he told me, about *who he once was*; she wanted to be a part of seeing him through to who he *would become.* That's how many of us need to approach our next step in life– without excuses. Whether you know it or not, your true voice is itching to come forth. It wants to return to what it was truly meant to be; and yours is different than mine or anyone else's. Don't let excuses justify a life of silence and stagnancy any longer.

Along with vocalizing comes what I believe is the most substantial realization on this journey: *it's already in you.* If we don't understand this, we'll find ourselves searching and searching in all the wrong places on an endless mission to uncover the treasure that is our unique expression. Whatever we glean from should enhance what is already in us, not give us an identity. Outside inspiration should help unlock our own inner, original flow of creativity. Don't think of creativity in terms of arts, invention, etc.; think of it in terms of something that originates from within you. We are all creative beings, in that we are individuals with our own voices, minds, and path; you are the only one that can do you. Half the battle of vocalizing is recognizing this very concept.

Another vital aspect of vocalizing may well be the most crucial to your morale: *speak positively.*

If all that is coming out of your mouth is doubt, fear, negativity, and the like, don't be surprised if those are the only things you reap. Don't look at this as some super-spiritual or anecdotal notion. It's only common sense that what you put out into the universe produces and reproduces itself. It can't do anything else. If it's bad, it produces bad. This is why a bad thought can become a lie, a lie can become hatred, hatred can become murder, and so on and so on. What are you saying about yourself? Are you putting yourself down? Stop saying you're not intelligent, or that you can't do something, or that you're not gifted enough. Say out loud that if anyone has the ability to accomplish anything, it's you! Say out loud that your life is worth just as much as anyone else. Use your own voice to your advantage and reshape your atmosphere. Positiveness will produce positiveness. It's a huge key to causing our entire world to change.

Now, don't be all crazy... Don't say stuff like, "I'm Chinese," if you are 100% Irish. That's not positive, that's delusional.

My wife once said to me during a difficult season in my life when I was complaining and rarely had a good thing to say, "I keep hearing you say what it is that you *don't* want; what about what you *do* want??" I'd been ranting, carrying on, and talking so much about what I didn't like or want that I hadn't ever taken the time to articulate what I truly would have wanted to see as a resolution. I think my mind was so focused on the negative aspects of my life during that time that I probably wasn't sure how I wanted to pursue that resolution. Once I started voicing possible solutions more than whining about the problem, the "light at the end of the tunnel" became more of a reality. I learned that my voice can either keep me inside of my own damnation or lead me into a broader, more hopeful place.

Make No Apologies!!!

Discovering your voice after not using it for so long is like striking oil– believe me, I know. Once this liberating quality awakens, you don't want to go back. A near guarantee, however, is that someone or something will arise to attempt to *shut it back down*. It almost seems like a law of nature: if it's rising, somethings got to push it down; if it's warming, somethings got to try to cool it... if it's beautifying, somethings got to try to uglify it. If we don't understand this, the likelihood of being blindsided and set back becomes a greater reality.

A better way to view it, I believe, is to see it as not only an attack against your voice or expression, but against *your life as a whole.*

Remember, your voice is an extension of your innards (hehe!); or your inner self, I should say. If something is threatening that, you've got to see it as attempted murder, because that's essentially what it is. Think of how "dead" you felt in that obscurity, that silence, or even in the comfort of that oblivion you didn't realize was entrapping you. Now think of the treasure, that diamond you find when you discover that freedom of expression, the freedom to create, the wildness of who you really are asserting itself into the atmosphere around it, as if it knows it's been missed for an eternity. Then... here come those voice raiders, ready to drag you back into darkness, to attack you with every weapon they have to cause you to believe that your voice really never was worth hearing, that your life doesn't really have a unique place in this world. They liked who you were before. They liked you better when they could control you.

In simple terms, the solution is to guard your gift with everything you have. And make no apologies for being who you are. We all need change in areas, sure. We could all use a little (or a lot) of help getting to our destination in life, but our voice is our voice. Understand that there is no amount of money, accolades, or anything else that is worth "selling your soul" for and losing your uniqueness. So if I face adversity because of my natural expression, and it's obvious that the tension is only there to destroy me and return me to silence, I either push back or move on; whichever the situation calls for. But I never make apology for being the pureness of what I was created to be. Of course, I express my regret for offending someone; or perhaps there was another way I could have said something, or whatever– that's not what I'm talking about. It's about the pressure we feel to return to silence when our voice is *under*valued or *de*valued. Again, guard it.

Here is a brief checklist to help you stay on track with actively using your voice and continually breaking free of oppressors:

Make a list of all of the negative things you've said about yourself. (NOT what others have said about you, because in the end, it's not relevant.) THEN:

Say– don't just think– SAY OUT LOUD whatever is the opposite of those things, i.e. "My voice IS worth hearing," or "I AM a good mother," or "I DO have what it takes to start this business." Don't be afraid to say whatever good thing comes to mind. "I'm NOT stupid. I AM beautiful."

Recognize the triggers that cause you to shrink back into a repressed state, and be intentional about using your pure expression as an offensive measure.

List every excuse you've given yourself to remain timid and ashamed of your true voice, then burn that list. :)

Stop speaking negatively. It's sabotage.

Understand that your voice, as it is today, is perfect, because it's yours. You're not trying to GET a voice– you already have one. It will get stronger and stronger, clearer and clearer, but it's already perfect.

119

Chapter 10
THE POWER OF THE VOICE

I've related my personal experiences many times throughout this book. There are many more stories I could tell, but I'm not the only one discovering the power in my own voice. There are countless others whose stories and experiences are much like my own, if not more impacting.

Like I said, hearing or learning about it is one thing; but becoming aware of its tangibility and attainability in one's own life is another. When we see a demonstration of what's being conveyed, it gives a good jolt to our ability to place our faith in the substance of that thing. I was excited during the course of writing and researching for this book to come across a few people whose lives and stories appeared to be a clear demonstration of what it is to come out of oblivion and into their freedom of expression. I found a story about singer who had been sexually abused as a child, and is now using that very experience as a piece of the platform she uses to give others coming out of abusive situations a place to release their voice. Instead of allowing that evil to dictate what the rest of her life should look like, she used her own voice to cause that trauma to work for her. Awesome. Check out www.tapology.org.

I was also encouraged to find Dan Cumberland, author of <u>The Meaning Manifesto</u> and the visionary behind "The Meaning Movement" (**www.themeaningmovement.com**), through which he helps others discover how to cause the fabric of who they are to tie into their endeavors, such as business, hobbies, etc. As I interviewed him, it became apparent to me that before he began to explore his true identity, he could have been the poster child for the "conformity clause" chapter of this book! He'd been advised to pursue bible school, then begin a career in ministry, so that's what he did. After he graduated from bible college, he began work as a youth pastor. But something wasn't quite right.

Dan began to question many things in his life during this time, feeling that even though he was supposedly walking in his "calling", the pieces just weren't fitting. The dissatisfaction and unrest even caused him to experience a level of depression. As he began to take inventory of his life, the question was posed: "Who told you that you were supposed to be a youth pastor?" This question disturbed him quite a bit, he said, but it began to challenge him to truly examine himself and why his life was in the state it was.

Over the course of time, he discovered that he had a desire to help others find their true identity. Working with the youth had helped him discover this part of himself, although he knew at this point that a pastor was not what he was supposed to be. So, he embarked on a journey to discover how to help others, the whole while discovering more and more about who he was. He returned to school to learn more about this new passion, earning a masters degree in interdisciplinary studies. He subsequently launched *The Meaning Movement*, began to write, meet with those who seek his help, speak at universities, and even run a photography company with his wife.

I believe it's important to understand that just because we begin to move in the direction of our true expression leading us onto our path, it doesn't mean that everything will be all glorious and wonderful from that point onward. It's not easy; but when you discover the power behind your true identity, nothing will be able to stop you. When Dan began his new endeavor, he questioned whether or not he was even capable of being this person he'd discovered on the inside; whether or not he could really make his business succeed. Although it's ideally courageous that we are willing to take the steps– or even risks– to become who we are meant to be, life and its demands don't just go away. In other words, the man had bills to pay; and life didn't care about whether he had found his voice. But when he decided that 1) this was who he was now, and 2) this was like and experiment *within* life; he didn't have to compromise his newly found power.

Another thing to see in this story is the fact that during the portion of Dan's life where he was dissatisfied and depressed, he was still developing his passion and skill to work with people. We've touched on this in earlier chapters. Although we don't always see it, everything on our path can be useful to our overall growth. If we'll open our eyes, we discover that most of our experiences add to the power of our voice. We tend not to "channel" these experiences because we don't recognize their value. Oh, but if we only knew how much more impact we could have by embracing everything we've ever walked through!

Another person I greatly respect is a woman who has also dedicated her life to helping and equipping others to be the most they can be, Barbara Wentroble. She and her husband spend much of their time in speaking engagements and working with their network of business people, doctors, ministers, teachers, and anyone else who desires to break out of the typical mold and model of their spheres and blossom into something they could never have imagined. She is one of the fieriest people I know. Her voice carries much weight in the arena in which she operates, and she is the *least* timid person one could ever meet. However, like many of us, she didn't start out that way. Here is an excerpt from her book "Rise to Your Destiny, Woman Of God":

> *...As a child, limitations were normal*
> *for me. I grew up in a home in which*

124

> *the maxim of children being seen and not heard was the order of the day. Even when I did not actually hear those words being spoken, the atmosphere was filled with the meaning. By the time I reached adulthood, I had learned to live in an environment in which I suppressed my feelings, opinions, and a way of vocalizing my thoughts. Because my words were restricted, I grew up believing that they were not important, and I soon developed a fear of speaking. I learned to live in a manner devoid of personal expression, feeling that I had nothing of value to offer.*

Oh, how I could relate when I read this! The wondrous thing about this is that if you were to meet her today, she is far from this person you just read about. Some may think, "Well of course, she's no longer a child. She has matured out of that mindset." Cute. The reason I'd have to strongly disagree is because I've known too many people, including myself, whose adult lives were resoundingly affected by the oppression imposed on them in their childhood years. Let's not even talk about suicide attempts, illegal activities, etc. So how did Barbara find the wherewithal to overcome her timidity and become the powerhouse that she is today?

She stated in this same book that she realized that she had signed an "unwritten contract" with everything that was designed to hold her back and keep her in a restricted place by allowing it to become a part of her psyche and lifestyle. So naturally, it only made sense that she'd have to work to *come out of agreement with it.* You have the power to break agreement with everything that wants to imprison you. If the "opposing force" is trying to force you to go left, then take the risk and go *right.* You'll at least send the message to your own soul that you aren't living under the oppression any longer. And let me reiterate... Barbara Wentroble is NOT that timid, suppressed person any longer. I've never known that person.

She also had to face her fears. She had to forgive. She had to be proactive about what she believed. She had to address her insecurities. Through all of the aforementioned examples, we've confirmed that we must be willing to examine ourselves, be willing to take risks, that we must embrace every part of our journey (even the parts we despise), and that it's imperative that we come out of agreement with everything that wants to restrict us and keep us in obscurity. Sound familiar?

A final thought, and a mention that is far too critical to pass over, is love. There are so many things I and others like me have walked through that without love, we'd have never succeeded. Receiving and giving love is a substance vital to the fabric of human life. I encourage those of you who have the opportunity to pour out love on someone who needs it, to do so. You don't know how deeply it serves the soul and speaks to an individual's value. The nurturing love of a mother literally balances a newborn's emotions and gives them a feeling of security in who he is to her. I also encourage you not to shun the love that is being shown to you. Don't hold on to the walls that have been built around your emotions and keep you from receiving love. It is a nourishment everyone was born needing, and it will, if you let it, free your expression.

Love is empowering. Ask former U.S. Secretary of State, Condoleeza Rice, who had a father and mother who loved her unconditionally and made her know who she was. Her father caused her to believe that she was capable of achieving whatever she aimed for. She eventually became the first female African American U.S. Secretary of State, among other prestigious titles and positions she has held over the years. Love is so much more than an emotion or feeling; it involves the limits someone will go to in order to see you be the best you that you can be. It involves a selflessness and perseverance that refuses to give up. We all need it; because without it, literally everything I've said in this book will end up being a bunch of heady words whose appropriation is nothing more than a scholarly attempt at addressing a rather spiritual issue. Love *is* power.

Thank you, Mrs. Vincent, for all of your love; your deep, true love for God causes you to love me in that same way. It empowers me.

Conclusion

Time wouldn't serve me to tell the stories of all the unlikely powerful, pivotal voices of the ages which, without them, the world would not turn; people like Helen Keller, deaf and blind since her toddler years, yet was an avid, influential writer, lecturer, and activist who is studied to this day. People like Martin Luther King, who kept speaking and boldly challenging injustice, even when his life was threatened. People like Malala Yousafzai, who because of her bold voice in the midst of oppression, discrimination, and attempted murder, became the youngest person ever to win the Nobel Prize. With a simple whisper, wars begin and end. With a shout or a subtle motion, an entire thought can be conveyed. And these are all from flesh-and-blood human beings just like you and me. Are they special? Yes! And so are we all. If we only knew who we were.

Your voice is more powerful than you realize. As the saying goes, you've been like a sleeping lion waiting to be awakened. How will your story sound? It's already begun; how will it end?

The same way there is no sound without movement, there is no movement without sound. Science will tell you that. On some level, one is always causing the other. The sound in you is being awakened to cause movement within you and around you. This stirring in you is strengthening your faith in yourself and what you believe. You are discovering the inherent purpose that has been ready to manifest. The path is yours; the story is yours. The voice is awake, and it's getting ready to roar...

Are you ready?

I'd rather be hated for who I am than loved for who I'm not.

~ Kurt Cobain

Your time is limited, so don't waste it living someone else's life. Don't be trapped by dogma- which is living with the results of other people's thinking. Don't let the noise of others' opinions drown out your own inner voice.

~Steve Jobs

If you hear a voice within you say, "You cannot paint," then by all means paint, and that voice will be silenced.

~Vincent Van Gogh

Love now, not later. Also, love later.

~Jarod Kintz

...The caged bird sings with a fearful trill
of things unknown but longed for still
and his tune is heard on the distant hill
for the caged bird sings of freedom.
~Maya Angelou

THE POWER OF

THE

VOICE

Made in the USA
Monee, IL
28 January 2024

52086174R00075